Merry Christmas
NOEL
M
ER
RY·CH
RISTM
AS
MERRY CHRISTMAS

Merry Christmas
MERRY CHRISTMAS
NOEL
MERRY CHRISTMAS

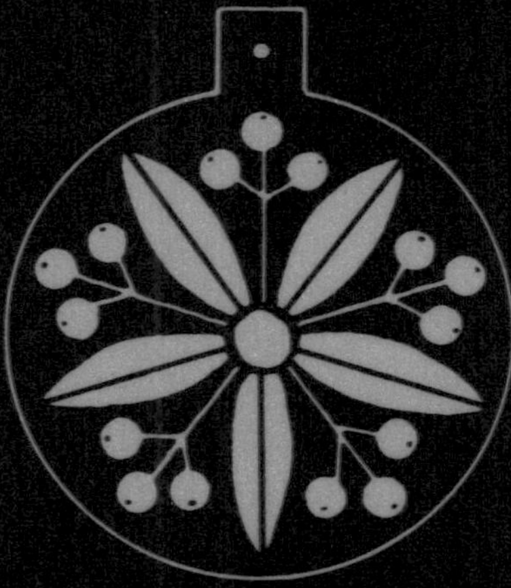

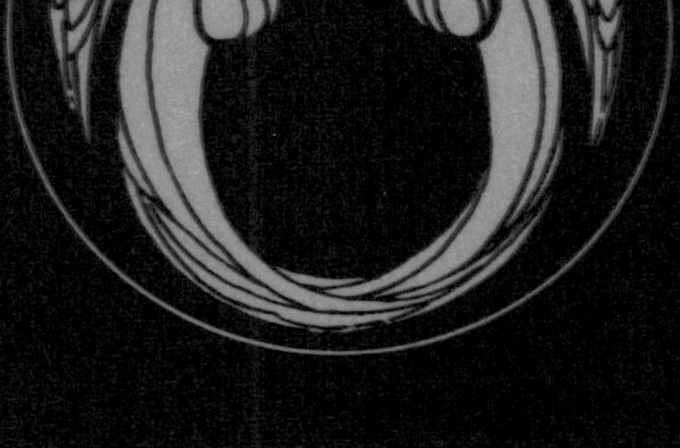

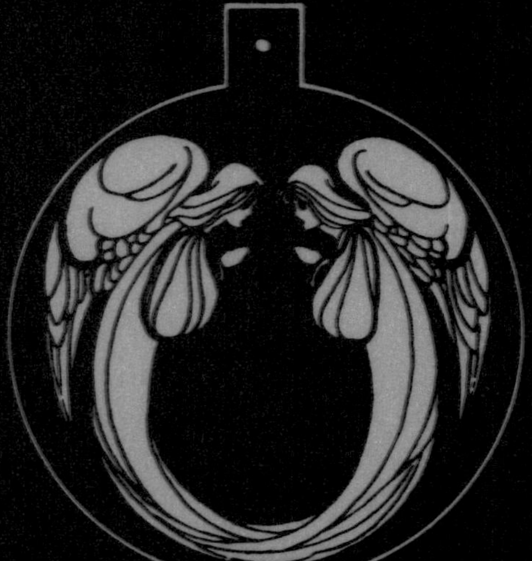

I BRING YOU
GLAD TIDINGS

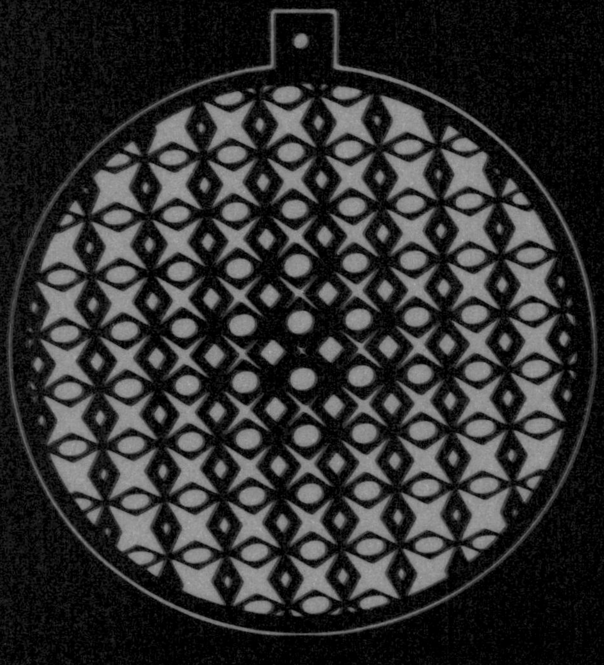

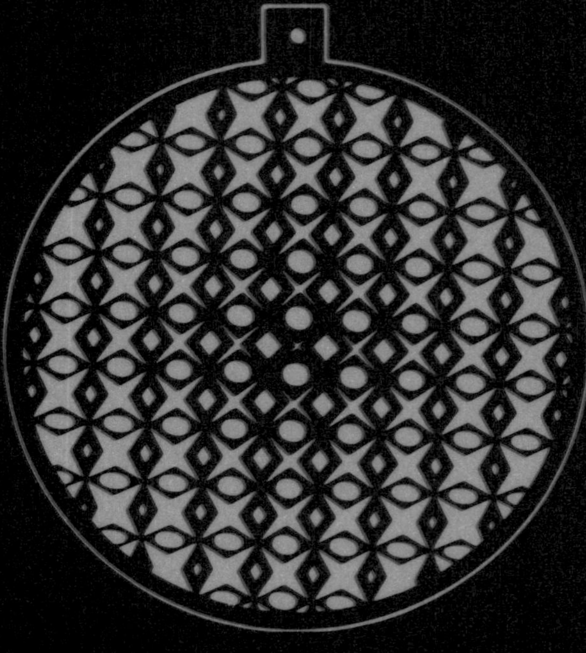

PEACE ON EARTH
NOEL
NOEL
GOOD WILL TO MEN

PEACE ON EARTH
NOEL
NOEL
GOOD WILL TO MEN

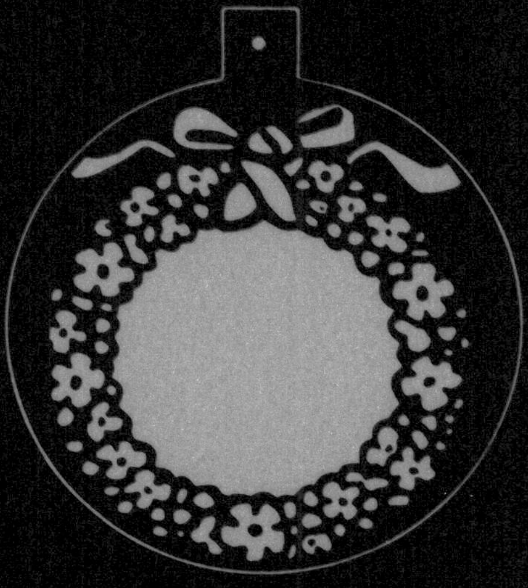